WHO IS JESUS?

THE WHIRRING CHILDREN SERIES - BOOK 1

ANTHONY MWANGI

Crony Trading LTD

All Scripture quotations are taken from the King James Version (KJV) of the Holy Bible.

This book is part of The Whirring Children™ Series, a gentle collection designed to help young hearts discover Jesus Christ with wonder, simplicity, and joy.

ISBN: 978-1-918186-15-4
Printed in the United Kingdom
First Edition — 2025

Every effort has been made to create content that is safe, tender, and aligned with Christian teaching.
This book is intended to support parents, teachers, and caregivers as they guide children in understanding the love of Jesus.

*To every child who opens this book
with bright eyes and a wondering heart—
may you always know
that Jesus sees you,
Jesus loves you,
and Jesus delights in the sound of your name.*

*And to the parents, teachers, and caregivers
who guide these little ones with patience and grace—
may His gentle presence fill every moment
you share together.*

*This book is for you,
with love and gratitude.*

— Anthony Mwangi

"Suffer the little children to come unto me, and forbid them not: for of such is the kingdom of God."
— Mark 10:14 (KJV)

JESUS CHRIST

CONTENTS

FOREWORD

Dear Parent, Teacher, or Caregiver,

Thank you for choosing to place this book in the hands of a child you love.
You are giving them one of the greatest gifts a young heart can receive; the chance to meet Jesus in a way that feels safe, simple, and deeply personal.

Children learn through wonder.
Through pictures in their imagination.
Through stories told slowly, gently, and with love.
This book is crafted to meet them there; in that sacred space where faith begins as a whisper
and grows into a steady light.

You will notice that every chapter invites your child:

- **to see Jesus with childlike eyes,**

- **to feel His kindness,**

- **to trust His nearness,**

- **and to speak to Him as naturally as they speak to you.**

The goal is not to rush information,
but to nurture connection.
A child who feels loved by Jesus
will want to know Him more.

As you read, pause often.

Ask simple questions.
Encourage imagination.
Let the child describe what they picture.
Let them linger in moments where Jesus feels close.

In these early years, faith is not shaped by explanation—
it is shaped by experience.
This book is written to create that experience:
the quiet miracle of a child realising,
"Jesus knows me. Jesus likes me. Jesus is with me."

May your shared reading moments become
memories your child carries forever—
and may the love of Jesus
fill your home, your heart,
and every chapter of the journey ahead.

With gratitude,
Anthony Mwangi

INTRODUCTION

Every great story begins with a meeting.
And the greatest story of all begins when a child discovers that Jesus has been near them from the very start.

This book is an invitation into that first meeting.
Not rushed.
Not complicated.
Just gentle steps into the warmth of a Friend who loves with a steady, never-ending love.

Inside these pages, children will see who Jesus is through simple stories, soft pictures, and everyday moments—moments they already understand. They will learn that He is the One who listens when they talk, smiles when they laugh, and stays beside them even when things feel hard.

Each chapter carries a single truth, wrapped in language a child can hold. The memory verse plants that truth in the heart. The short prayer gives it a voice. And the "Talk With Jesus" moment helps children learn to speak with Him as naturally as they speak to someone they love.

This book is the beginning of a journey—one filled with kindness, courage, and the steady glow of God's presence. My prayer is that every child who opens these pages will feel seen, treasured, and deeply safe in the arms of God even Jesus.

Let's begin the adventure together.

PREFACE

This little book began with a simple longing: *to help a child hear the gentle whisper of Jesus early, clearly, and joyfully.* In a world that moves fast and speaks loudly, children often sense God before they understand Him. Their hearts notice warmth before they recognise presence. Their spirits lean toward love before they have a name for it.

This series was created to honour that sacred beginning. Each page, each prayer, each small activity invites a child to meet Jesus the way He loves to be met—simply, trustingly, and without fear. No pressure. No performance. Just a quiet doorway where a child can step into the story of God and discover that they already belong.

The vision is forward-facing: to raise children who know Jesus not only as a name in a book, but as a friend who sits with them, listens to them, celebrates them, and steadies them. A generation confident in His nearness becomes a generation bold in His love.

If this book helps a child whisper, "Jesus, I know You are here," then the mission is already succeeding. May these early steps in faith grow into a lifelong walk filled with wonder.

With gratitude, hope, and joy for every little heart beginning this journey—
Anthony Mwangi

PROLOGUE

Before a child learns to read a story,
their heart is already listening for one.

Somewhere in the quiet moments
in the hush before bedtime,
in the giggle of playtime,
in the soft comfort of a parent's arms
a small voice begins to wonder:

"Who is Jesus?"

And long before that question is spoken,
Jesus has already been whispering an answer.
He has been near from the beginning
steadier than a heartbeat,
brighter than a sunrise,
closer than a favorite blanket tucked under the chin.

This book opens the door to that nearness.

It is not a big door.
It does not swing with noise or hurry.
It is a little door
just the right size for little hands,
little steps,
and little hearts learning big truths.

Through these pages, children begin their first walk with Jesus
a gentle walk,
a safe walk,

a walk filled with wonder and belonging.

Here, they will meet the One who loves first,
loves always,
and loves them more than they can ever imagine.

Let the journey begin.

PART I

MEETING JESUS

CHAPTER 1

A FRIEND WHO KNOWS MY NAME

Discovering that Jesus sees, knows, and loves every child personally.

Before you ever learned to walk...
before you learned to laugh...
before you even opened your eyes for the very first time...
Jesus already knew your name.

He whispered it with joy.
He held it like a treasure.
He carried it in His heart as a promise.

Your name is not just a sound.
It is a song Jesus sings over you.

He saw you before anyone else did.
He dreamed of the kindness that would grow in your heart.
He imagined the courage that would rise inside you when life felt scary.
He knew the way your smile would light up the world.
He knew every part of you and He loved every part.

Nothing about you is hidden from Him.
Not your thoughts.
Not your feelings.
Not your secrets.
Not your worries.
Not your hopes.

Jesus knows you so well that He can hear your heart even when you don't say a word.

And still — He wants you to talk to Him.

Because He is not just the King of Heaven.
He is not just the One who made the oceans, mountains, and stars.
He is not just the One who keeps the whole world spinning.

He is also your Friend.

A friend who never gets tired of listening.
A friend who understands your tears.
A friend who celebrates your victories.
A friend who sits beside you even when you feel alone.
A friend who stays near even when everyone else walks away.

Jesus does not wait for you to be perfect.
He does not wait for you to be older.
He does not wait for you to be brave or strong.

He comes close **now**.

Close enough to hear your whisper.
Close enough to catch your sigh.
Close enough to wrap your heart in peace.

And every time you speak His name, something gentle stirs in the air
a warmth, a knowing, a quiet joy
because Jesus loves hearing your voice.

He knows your name.
He loves your name.
And when you say His name, He knows exactly who you are.

Child's Declaration

"Jesus knows my name, loves my heart, and is always close to me."

Short. Strong. Repeatable. A seed of identity planted in the child's spirit.

Memory Verse

> *"I have called thee by thy name; thou art mine." — Isaiah 43:1 (KJV)*

This is the perfect anchor for this chapter — intimate, reassuring, beautiful.

Prayer

Jesus, thank You for calling me by my name.
Thank You that I belong to You.
Help me feel Your love every day,
and remind me that You are always close to me.

Amen.

CHAPTER 2

BEFORE THE STARS
LEARNED TO SHINE

Jesus existed before everything and still chooses to be close to us.

Before the first sunrise warmed the sky...
before the moon learned how to glow...
before the stars were sprinkled like tiny lamps in the night...

Jesus already was.

He didn't begin.
He didn't grow into being.
He didn't appear out of nowhere.

He has **always** been.

He was with God the Father.
He was full of light.
He was full of life.
He was full of love.

Jesus was there when the world was quiet and empty
before the rivers ran,
before the grass grew,
before the birds sang,
before the oceans danced,
before any heart ever beat.

With His voice, worlds happened.

With His word, mountains rose.
With His breath, everything living began to breathe.

But here is the most wonderful part:

Even though Jesus made the whole universe
even though He holds galaxies in His hands
even though angels bow before Him in shining worship

He still chooses to come close to you.

He chooses to listen to your small thoughts.
He chooses to hold your tiny fears.
He chooses to notice your quiet joys.
He chooses to walk beside you even when no one else sees you.

The same Jesus who existed before time began
is the Jesus who sits with you
when you are drawing, singing, learning, resting, or dreaming.

He is older than the stars…
brighter than the sun…
and yet gentle enough to whisper peace into a child's heart.

Jesus is big — bigger than anything.
But His love knows how to get small enough
so you can feel it up close.

He made the stars…
but He chooses **you**.

• Child's Declaration

"Jesus is bigger than the whole world, but He stays close to me."

Memory Verse

"Before Abraham was, I am." — John 8:58 (KJV)

Simple. Eternal. Majestic.

It reveals Jesus as the One who has no beginning.

Prayer

Jesus, You were here before everything,
and You are here with me right now.
Thank You for being big and strong,
and thank You for staying close to my heart.
Help me remember that You never change.

Amen.

CHAPTER 3

THE WHISPER THAT MAKES JESUS SMILE

Learning that talking to Jesus is simple, safe, and natural.

Some people think you must speak loudly for God to hear.
Some think you must use fancy words.
Some think you must wait for the "right moment."

But Jesus listens differently.

He hears the softest whisper.
He hears the quietest thought.
He hears what your heart says
even when your mouth says nothing at all.

When you talk to Jesus,
you don't have to be grown-up,
or perfect,
or brave,
or strong.

You just have to be **you**.

If you are happy, tell Him.
If you are sad, tell Him.
If you are scared, tell Him.
If you are confused, tell Him.
If you are thankful, tell Him.

If you don't know what to say at all...
sit with Him quietly
and He will sit with you.

Jesus loves your voice.
He loves the sound of your heart speaking.
He loves when you come close
just to share a moment with Him.

Your whisper travels straight to Him.
It never gets lost.
It never gets ignored.
It never gets pushed aside.

Every whisper is a gift.
Every word is a treasure.
Every little prayer makes Jesus smile.

Because talking to Him
isn't a rule to follow
it's a friendship to enjoy.

When you stop for even one second
and say,
"Jesus, I love You..."
or
"Jesus, help me..."
or
"Jesus, be near..."
He turns His heart toward you
with joy,
with kindness,
with warmth.

You don't have to shout to Heaven.
Heaven leans toward you
the moment you speak.

Talking to Jesus is simple.

It's safe.
It's natural.
It's home.

Child's Declaration

"Jesus hears me every time I talk to Him even my whisper."

Memory Verse

> *"Draw nigh to God, and he will draw nigh to you."*
> *—James 4:8 (KJV)*

Clear. Comforting. Close.

Prayer

Jesus, thank You for hearing me
even when I talk softly.
Thank You for coming close
every time I whisper Your name.
Help my heart stay near You
in every moment of my day.
Amen.

PART II

GOD'S LOVE IN JESUS

THE
WHIRRING
CHILDREN

CHAPTER 4

WHY JESUS CAME

Understanding God's love made visible through His Son.

Long before you were born,
long before your parents were born,
long before anyone alive today ever breathed their first breath…
God had a plan.

A love plan.
A rescue plan.
A "bring-My-children-close-to-Me" plan.

And at the centre of that plan
was Jesus.

God wanted the world to know His heart
a heart full of kindness,
full of mercy,
full of goodness,
full of light.

So He sent Jesus
not to frighten us,
not to judge us,
not to stay far away…
but to show us what God's love looks like
with hands,
and feet,

and a smile.

Jesus came to make God easy to see.
Easy to understand.
Easy to come close to.

When Jesus walked on the earth,
He showed us exactly what God feels:
He feels close.
He feels gentle.
He feels warm.
He feels like home.

Jesus came so every child — including you
could know without any doubt:

"God loves me."
"God wants me."
"God will never leave me."

He came to shine light into darkness,
peace into fear,
hope into sadness,
and joy into every heart willing to receive Him.

Jesus is God's love made real,
made touchable,
made near.

That's why He came, for you.

Child's Declaration

"God loves me so much that He sent Jesus for me."

Memory Verse

> *"For God so loved the world, that he gave his only begotten Son..."*

—John 3:16 (KJV)

Prayer

Father, thank You for loving the world.
Thank You for loving me.
Thank You for sending Jesus
so I could know Your heart.
Help me remember Your love every day.
Amen.

CHAPTER 5

THE LOVE THAT WALKED AMONG US

How Jesus treated people, especially children, with gentleness and kindness.

When Jesus walked through villages and towns,
people hurried just to see Him.
Mothers carried their babies.
Fathers lifted their children onto their shoulders.
Grandparents leaned on canes and smiled with hope.

Everyone wanted to come close
because Jesus made people feel safe.

He never pushed anyone away.
He never turned anyone aside.
He never said, "You aren't important."

Instead, He stooped down.
He listened carefully.
He touched gently.
He spoke softly.
He looked into people's eyes
and made them feel known.

When children ran toward Him,
some grown-ups tried to stop them.
But Jesus said,
"Let them come."

He opened His arms wide.
He welcomed them with joy.
He blessed them with love.
He made them feel like the most important people in the whole crowd.

To Jesus, every child mattered.
Every tear mattered.
Every smile mattered.
Every hurt, every hope, every dream
He cared about it all.

Jesus didn't just teach love.
He **walked** love.
He **spoke** love.
He **showed** love in every step He took.

And He still does.
You are one of the children He opens His arms to.
You are one of the little ones He blesses.
You are one He calls precious.

The love that walked among the people long ago
walks beside you
today.

Child's Declaration

"Jesus welcomes me with open arms."

Memory Verse

> *"Suffer the little children to come unto me... for of such is the kingdom of God."*
> *— Mark 10:14 (KJV)*

Prayer

Jesus, thank You for welcoming children,
and thank You for welcoming me.
Help me feel Your arms around me
and Your love inside me.
Amen.

CHAPTER 6

THE WAY JESUS LOVED EVERYONE

Stories of compassion, healing, listening, and welcoming.

Everywhere Jesus went,
He brought love with Him
not just for some people,
but for **everyone**.

He loved the ones who were hurting.
He loved the ones who were lonely.
He loved the ones others avoided.
He loved the ones no one else understood.
He loved the ones who made mistakes.

Jesus walked into places where people felt forgotten
and reminded them they were seen.

He listened to stories others never heard.
He touched hands others wouldn't touch.
He healed bodies that were sick.
He calmed hearts that were afraid.
He lifted faces that were bowed down.
He gave hope to people who thought hope was gone.

Jesus loved with a love
that did not stop,
did not shrink,
did not run away.

And that same love
is reaching toward you.

His compassion is for you.
His patience is for you.
His kindness is for you.
His listening heart is for you.
His healing touch is for you.

Jesus loved everyone then
and He loves you now
with that very same love.

Child's Declaration

Memory Verse

"We love him, because he first loved us." — *1 John 4:19 (KJV)*

Prayer

Jesus, thank You for loving me first.
Teach me how to love others like You love.
Fill my heart with Your kindness
so I can share it with the world.

Amen.

PART III

JESUS SAVES AND LIVES FOREVER

THE
WHIRRING
CHILDREN
Learning God's Love, One Whirl at a Time

CHAPTER 7

THE DAY LOVE GAVE EVERYTHING

Jesus giving His life on the cross.

Before the world ever learned to say His name, Jesus carried a love too big to measure.
He walked among people who didn't always understand Him, but He never stopped loving them.
He healed the hurting.
He lifted the lonely.
He listened to children with a smile that made them feel seen.
And then came the day when love stepped into its greatest moment.

Soldiers took Jesus away.
Crowds shouted.
The sky grew heavy.
But Jesus did not run.
He did not fight back.
He carried a cross He didn't deserve because *we* were the ones He loved.

He thought of every child; every laugh, every tear, every dream, every fear.
He thought of children who hadn't even been born yet.
He carried their worries in His heart and walked forward.

When nails pierced His hands, love did not stop.
When darkness covered the land, love did not hide.

When people walked away, love remained.

Jesus gave everything not because people were perfect,
but because His love is perfect.

He chose the cross because He wanted every child to know:
"Nothing can ever take you away from My love."

The cross was not the end.
It was the door.
A door Jesus opened with His own life so the world could walk into
God's forever-love.

Child's Declaration

"Jesus loves me so much that He gave everything for me, and His
love will never leave me."

Memory Verse

"Christ died for us." — Romans 5:8 KJV

Prayer

"Jesus, thank You for loving me with Your whole heart.
Thank You for giving Your life so I can belong to God forever.
Help me understand Your love more each day.

Amen."

CHAPTER 8

STRONGER THAN DARKNESS

Why Jesus died and why His love wins.

Darkness tries to whisper lies.
It says, "You are alone."
It says, "You are not good enough."
It says, "God is far away."

But darkness is small compared to Jesus.

When Jesus died on the cross, He wasn't losing.
He was fighting for us in a battle only He could win.

He carried every lie darkness ever whispered.
He carried every fear.
He carried every sin.
He took it all to the cross and said, "No more."

The moment Jesus breathed His last, the whole earth felt it.
The ground shook.
The rocks broke.
The thick curtain in the Temple tore from top to bottom as if Heaven itself shouted,
"The way is open! Come close! Don't be afraid!"

Jesus didn't die to make us sad.
He died to make us **free**.

Free from fear.

Free from shame.
Free from the shadows that try to chase us.

When Jesus rose again, darkness realised something it hoped was never true:

Love is stronger.
Light is stronger.
Jesus is stronger.

Children don't have to fight darkness alone.
They carry Jesus' light—a light darkness cannot understand, cannot stop, and cannot put out.

Child's Declaration

"Jesus' light lives in me, and darkness can never win against Him."

Memory Verse

> *"The light shineth in darkness; and the darkness comprehended it not." —John 1:5 KJV*

Prayer

"Jesus, thank You for shining Your light in my life.
When I feel afraid, help me remember that You are stronger.
Let Your love be my courage every day.

Amen."

CHAPTER 9

THE MORNING THAT CHANGED THE WORLD

Jesus rising again, alive forever.

It was early morning.
The sky was gray.
The world was quiet, as if holding its breath.

Women walked toward Jesus' tomb with heavy hearts.
They thought everything was over.
They thought the story had ended.

But God was writing a new chapter.

When they reached the tomb, the stone wasn't closed.
It was rolled away.
The guards were gone.
And inside… Jesus wasn't there.

Before fear could rise, an angel spoke:
"He is not here: for He is risen."
Light filled their hearts.
Hope rushed back like the sunrise breaking open the sky.

That same morning, Jesus appeared alive, smiling, strong.
He walked with His friends.
He talked with them.
He let them touch His hands to know it was really Him.

Death had lost.
Hope had won.
Jesus was alive forever.

And the world changed.

Now every child can wake up each morning knowing:
Jesus lives today.
He listens.
He speaks.
He walks with them.
He never leaves.

Because the tomb is empty, children can dream of a future filled with light.
Because Jesus is alive, their hearts can be brave.
Because Jesus lives forever, they can know Him forever.

Child's Declaration

"Jesus is alive forever, and He walks with me every day."

Memory Verse

"He is not here: for He is risen." — Matthew 28:6 KJV

Prayer

"Jesus, thank You for rising again and filling the world with hope.
Help me feel Your presence today.
Stay close to me as I learn, play, and grow.
Let Your joy live in my heart forever.

Amen."

PART IV

JESUS LOVES ME

THE
WHIRRING
CHILDREN

CHAPTER 10

JESUS IS ALWAYS WITH ME

Learning Jesus is close in every moment.

Sometimes the world feels big.
Classrooms feel loud.
Bedrooms feel quiet.
Fields feel wide.
And hearts feel small.

But Jesus is never far.

He walks with children in ways they can feel
like peace in their chest,
like a soft thought that says "I'm here,"
like a warm feeling when they pray,
like a gentle courage when they try something new.

A child can whisper His name in the middle of a busy playground,
and Jesus hears them as if they were the only one speaking.

A child can talk to Him while lying in bed in the deep stillness of
night,
and Jesus listens as though the whole world paused just for that
moment.

He is there in the laughter of friends.
He is there in the quiet steps walking home.
He is there when a child feels brave
and when they don't.

Jesus doesn't wait for perfect moments.
He steps into every moment.

He is the Friend who keeps pace with tiny feet,
the Shepherd who watches with patient eyes,
the Saviour who never loses sight of His children.

And the more a child learns to notice Him,
the more they realise:
Jesus is not far away.
Jesus is right here.
Everywhere.
Always.

Child's Declaration

"Jesus is with me all the time. I am never alone."

Memory Verse

"I am with you always." — Matthew 28:20 KJV

Prayer

"Jesus, thank You for being close to me in every moment.
Help me feel Your presence today.
Walk with me, stay with me, and remind me You are always near.

Amen."

CHAPTER 11

JESUS LOVES ME COMPLETELY

Understanding unconditional love.

Some love grows today and shrinks tomorrow.
Some love is loud one minute and quiet the next.
Some love depends on moods, moments, or mistakes.

But Jesus' love does not change.

Jesus loves children when they are smiling
and when they are crying.
He loves them when they get everything right
and when they don't understand at all.
He loves them when they run fast
and when they are tired and slow.
He loves them when their hearts feel strong
and when they feel confused, worried, or unsure.

His love is whole.
Complete.
Unbroken.
Bigger than the sky.
Stronger than time.

Jesus doesn't love children *because* they are perfect.
He loves them because **they are His.**

He made their hearts.
He knows their dreams.

He sees their future.
He knows the song inside their soul that has not yet learned its melody.

He loves them when they pray.
He loves them when they forget to pray.
He loves them when they feel close.
He loves them when they feel far.

Nothing a child does can make Jesus love them more.
Nothing a child does can make Him love them less.

His love is not a river that dries up.
It is an ocean that never ends.

Child's Declaration

"Jesus loves all of me, all the time, and His love never stops."

Memory Verse

"We love him, because he first loved us." — 1 John 4:19 KJV

Prayer

"Jesus, thank You for loving me completely.
Help me feel Your love every day,
and help me share Your love with others. Amen."

CHAPTER 12

JESUS LOVES ME ON
EVERY KIND OF DAY

Good days, hard days, quiet days, growing days.

Some days feel bright
when the sun shines,
the games go well,
and everything feels simple.

Some days feel heavy
when nothing works,
when tears come suddenly,
or when hearts feel tired for reasons children can't explain.

Some days feel slow
quiet hours,
long thoughts,
wondering what comes next.

Some days feel exciting
new places,
new lessons,
new steps that make their heart beat fast.

And Jesus is in all of them.

On **good days**, Jesus celebrates with children.
He laughs with them.

He smiles in their joy.
He walks beside them as they explore the world with fearless excitement.

On **hard days**, Jesus sits close.
He wipes tears before they fall.
He puts peace into their breathing.
He whispers courage into their hearts:
"You are safe. You are Mine."

On **quiet days**, Jesus becomes the stillness.
He fills the silence with gentle comfort.
He gives children space to rest, to grow, to dream.

On **growing days**, Jesus steps in front and says,
"Come with Me. I'll help you learn."
And He gives them strength
not all at once,
but perfectly in time.

There is no day Jesus will not walk into.
No moment He will not fill.
No season He will not hold in His hands.

Every day belongs to Him.
And every child belongs to Him too.

Child's Declaration

"Jesus loves me on every kind of day, and He stays with me through all of them."

Memory Verse

> *"Casting all your care upon him; for he careth for you."* — *1 Peter 5:7 KJV*

Prayer

"Jesus, thank You for loving me on good days, hard days, quiet days, and growing days.
Teach me to trust You in every moment.
Walk with me in every day You give me. Amen."

PART V

MY FIRST STEPS WITH JESUS

THE
WHIRRING
CHILDREN
Learning God's Love, One Whirl at a Time

CHAPTER 13

MY FIRST MEMORY VERSE

1 John 4:19 — "We love Him, because He first loved us."

This is the first verse many children remember
because it answers one of the biggest questions in a child's heart:

"Why does Jesus love me?"

The verse tells them something simple and beautiful:
Jesus loved you first.

Before you ever prayed,
before you ever sang,
before you ever learned His name,

Jesus already loved you.

He loved you when you were tiny.
He loved you when you could not walk or speak.
He loved you before you were even born.
He loved you before you took your very first breath.

And because Jesus loved first,
your heart learns how to love Him back.

Imagine this verse like a small light inside the heart
a warm, gentle glow that never goes out.
Every time a child whispers it,

the light grows bigger, brighter, softer, stronger.

This is why memory verses matter:
They plant truth inside the heart,
and truth grows like a tree that stands even in the wind.

Child's Declaration

"Jesus loved me first. His love helps me love Him too."

Memory Verse

"We love him, because he first loved us." — 1 John 4:19 KJV

Prayer

"Jesus, thank You for loving me before I even knew You.
Help this verse stay in my heart forever.
Let Your love shine inside me every day. Amen."

CHAPTER 14

MY FIRST PRAYER OF BELONGING

A simple prayer that welcomes Jesus' love into a child's heart.

A child's first real prayer isn't fancy.
It isn't long.
It isn't full of big words.

It is honest.
It is gentle.
It is beautiful.

It sounds like a small knock on a big door
and Jesus always opens.

Sometimes children think they need to say the "right" things, but
Jesus only wants them to say **true** things.

A child might whisper,
"Jesus, I'm here."
or
"Jesus, I want You."
or
"Jesus, stay with me."

And Heaven hears it louder than thunder.

This prayer is called the **prayer of belonging**
because it tells Jesus,
"I am Yours, and I want You to be mine."

Not because a child is perfect.
Not because a child knows everything.
But because Jesus made their heart a home, He loves to enter.

This prayer becomes a doorway.
When a child speaks it,
Jesus gently steps inside.
He fills them with peace.
He fills them with joy.
He gives them a place in His family — forever.

Here is a simple prayer every child can say:

Prayer of Belonging

"Jesus, I love You because You love me.
Thank You for being my Saviour and my Friend.
Come into my heart and stay with me.
I belong to You, and You belong to me.

Amen."

Child's Declaration

"Jesus lives in my heart, and I belong to Him forever."

Memory Verse

"Behold, I stand at the door, and knock." — Revelation 3:20 KJV

CHAPTER 15

DAILY "TALK WITH JESUS" TIME

A child-friendly guide to talking with Jesus every day.

Talking with Jesus is not hard.
It doesn't need a special room, a special chair, or special words.
It doesn't need a long prayer or a perfect sentence.

Talking with Jesus is like talking to the warmest, kindest Friend.

Jesus listens in the morning when eyes are sleepy.
Jesus listens at school when thoughts feel busy.
Jesus listens on playgrounds when hearts feel joyful.
Jesus listens in the evening when shadows grow long.
Jesus listens at night when children curl beneath their blankets.

A child's prayer does not have to be loud.
Jesus hears whispers.
Jesus hears thoughts.
Jesus hears tiny words that flutter out like butterflies.

Here are gentle steps for a child's daily "Talk With Jesus" time:

1. Sit or stand or lie down — however you feel comfortable.

Jesus doesn't mind your posture.
He minds your heart.

2. Breathe slowly.

Feel Jesus near.
Imagine Him sitting beside you,
smiling softly,
happy to hear your voice.

3. Tell Him one thing you are thankful for.

A Bible.
A friend.
A moment.
A good meal.
A new lesson.
A sunny day.

Thanksgiving opens the heart.

4. Tell Him one thing that worries you.

A fear.
A question.
A feeling you don't understand.
A moment that hurt.

He cares about every small thing.

5. Ask Him to be with you today.

Ask Him to guide your steps,
help your heart,
protect your mind,
and walk with you.

6. Sit quietly for a few moments.

Let your heart be still.
This is when Jesus whispers.
Not with words a child hears with their ears,
but with peace a child feels inside.

Child's Declaration

"I can talk to Jesus every day. He listens to me and stays with me."

Memory Verse

"Pray without ceasing." — 1 Thessalonians 5:17 KJV

Prayer

"Jesus, thank You that I can talk to You anytime.
Help me hear Your gentle whispers and feel Your nearness.
Walk with me today.
Amen."

PART VI

GROWING WITH JESUS

CHAPTER 16

A LITTLE THANKFUL HEART

Helping kids practice gratitude.

Some mornings begin quietly, like the world is still waking up. The sun stretches. The birds whisper. And in the middle of all that softness, a little heart begins to stir — *your* heart.

Jesus watches over you before you even open your eyes. He sees your dreams, your yawns, your sleepy smile. And He whispers gently,
"I'm here. Let's begin this day together."

A thankful heart grows when it learns to notice small things — warm blankets... the smell of breakfast... the way light slips through your window... your family's voices... your own little breath.

And Jesus smiles when you see these gifts and treasure them.

He doesn't ask for a long list.
He loves the little things you tell Him.

You might say:

- "Thank You for my feet that can run."

- "Thank You for the sky that's so big."

- "Thank You for love that never leaves."

Every thank-you grows your heart stronger — like watering a tiny seed that knows it will someday become a tall, singing tree.

Jesus kneels beside you in the small moments and says, *"Keep noticing. Keep thanking. Your heart is becoming bright."*

Child's Declaration

"Jesus, You give me gifts every day. My heart sees them, treasures them, and says thank You."

Memory Verse

1 Thessalonians 5:18 KJV — "In every thing give thanks."

Prayer

"Jesus, help me see the gifts You place in my day. Make my heart thankful, even for tiny things. I want to notice Your love everywhere."

CHAPTER 17

JESUS HELPS ME WHEN I'M AFRAID

Encouraging courage through Christ's presence.

Everyone feels afraid sometimes even brave kids, even grown-ups, even kings in big stories of old. Fear can be loud like thunder... or small like a shadow in the corner... or sudden like a door creaking at night.

But Jesus never leaves His children in the dark.

Imagine this:
You are standing in a room that feels too quiet. The air is still. Your heart thumps. And then soft as a warm hand Jesus steps beside you.

You don't always see Him with your eyes, but you feel Him in your heart.
His nearness is like a light you can't turn off.

He whispers,
"Don't be scared. I am right here. I go nowhere without you."

Fear begins to shrink when Jesus becomes bigger in your thoughts.
Your imagination becomes a doorway, not to fear, but to the One who conquers fear with love.

Think of Jesus holding your hand.
Think of Him wrapping you in His peace.

Think of Him standing between you and every dark thing.

His presence turns trembling into courage,
and shaking knees into steady steps.

Child's Declaration

"When I feel afraid, Jesus is with me. His love makes me brave."

Memory Verse

Psalm 56:3 KJV — "What time I am afraid, I will trust in thee."

Prayer

"Jesus, stay close when I feel scared. Make my heart strong. Help me trust that You are with me in every dark and quiet place."

CHAPTER 18

JESUS GOES WITH ME EVERYWHERE

School, home, playtime, bedtime.

There is no place your feet can walk where Jesus does not walk too.
He is not limited like we are.
He doesn't get tired.
He doesn't need a map.
He doesn't wait outside any door.

Where you go — He goes.

Jesus at Home

When you're eating breakfast, He sits with you.
When you play, He smiles at your joy.
When you rest, He watches over you like a gentle shepherd guarding His lamb.

Jesus at School

He sits beside you at your desk.
He helps your thoughts when your mind feels slow.
He stays with you during noisy days and quiet hallways.

If someone is unkind, He whispers strength.
If someone is lonely, He nudges your heart to notice.

Jesus at Play

He delights in your laughter.

He runs with you on the playground.
He stands near you when you try something new and brave.

Jesus at Bedtime

When the lights go off, His presence stays on.
His peace settles around you like a soft blanket.
His love guards your dreams.

He whispers,
"I stay with you through the night, and I rise with you in the morning."

Jesus is not far.
Jesus is not busy.
Jesus is never too tired or distracted.
He is the friend who stays — everywhere, always.

Child's Declaration

"Jesus goes with me wherever I go. I am never alone."

Memory Verse

Matthew 28:20 KJV — "Lo, I am with you alway."

Prayer

"Jesus, thank You for walking with me in every place. Help me feel Your presence at home, school, while playing, and when I sleep."

PART VII

SPECIAL PAGES

THE
WHIRRING
CHILDREN

CHAPTER 19

JESUS LOVES ME — MY DECLARATION PAGE

A short, powerful identity statement for children.

Before the world knew your name, Jesus did.
Before you ever spoke a word, Jesus was singing over you.
Before you learned to walk, Jesus was already walking beside you.

This declaration page is a quiet space —
a place where your heart can stand tall
and say out loud who you are because Jesus loves you.

Read these words slowly.
Let them settle like sunshine inside you.
Let them become part of your breathing... your dreaming... your growing.

My Declaration

"Jesus loves me.
Jesus knows me.
Jesus stays with me.
I am never alone.
My heart belongs to Him,
and He delights in who I am.
I am loved in the morning.
I am loved at night.
I am loved on happy days

and loved on difficult days.
Jesus is my friend forever."

When you speak these words, Jesus leans close.
He places His peace inside your chest —
warm, brave, steady —
so you can carry His love wherever you go.

Memory Verse

Psalm 139:14 KJV — "I will praise thee; for I am fearfully and wonderfully made."

Prayer

"Jesus, thank You that You made me wonderfully, and You love me completely. Let Your love fill my heart every day."

CHAPTER 20

IF I WANT TO KNOW JESUS MORE...

Gentle next steps for young hearts beginning their faith journey.

Your journey with Jesus is like a growing garden
a little seed planted in soft soil,
reaching patiently toward the sun.

You don't have to hurry.
You don't have to understand everything at once.
Jesus celebrates every tiny step you take.

Here are simple ways to walk closer with Him
ways even a small child can follow,
with joy, with wonder, with confidence.

1. Talk to Jesus Anywhere

You can whisper to Him while brushing your teeth,
while tying your shoes,
while drawing,
while sitting in the car.
He listens to your softest words.

2. Tell Him About Your Day

Tell Him what made you laugh.
Tell Him what made you sad.
Tell Him what you don't understand.

Jesus loves your stories
even the short ones.

3. Read a Little Scripture

Even one verse is enough.
One verse can be a lamp.
One verse can be a hug.
One verse can be a seed that grows courage.

4. Listen With Your Heart

Sometimes Jesus speaks as a warm thought.
Sometimes as a peaceful feeling.
Sometimes through someone's kindness.
Sometimes through a verse that sticks to your heart.

5. Imagine Walking With Him

Picture Him beside you
smiling, gentle, safe.
Picture Him sitting at your table,
or holding your hand on your way to school.

Imagination opens a window
so your heart can see His closeness.

6. Ask Him to Help You Love Others

When you share, when you forgive,
when you choose kindness
your heart becomes a mirror
that reflects Jesus to the world.

Child's Declaration

"I can know Jesus more every day. My heart is open, my steps are small but strong, and Jesus guides me gently."

Memory Verse

James 4:8 KJV — "Draw nigh to God, and he will draw nigh to you."

Prayer

"Jesus, help me take little steps toward You every day. Make my heart close to Yours."

CHAPTER 21

A gentle roadmap for helping children meet Jesus, know His love, and walk with Him daily.

This guide is designed to help you carry the message of this book into a child's everyday world.
The goal is simple:
give them a living picture of Jesus — warm, near, patient, and strong — and guide them into a relationship that grows like a planted seed.

Each part of this guide is written to help you open space, open imagination, and open conversation.

1. THE HEART OF THIS BOOK

This book introduces Jesus in a way children can embrace:

- Jesus knows their name.

- Jesus is near and gentle.

- Jesus loves first.

- Jesus listens.

- Jesus is alive and active today.

• Jesus wants friendship with every child.

Your role is not to "teach lessons," but to **create moments** where the truth can settle naturally into their heart.

Children remember moments more than explanations.

2. HOW TO READ THIS BOOK WITH A CHILD

Think *slow*, *soft*, and *present*.

You don't need long sessions.
Small minutes done consistently matter more.

Here's a recommended flow:

• 1. Settle the space.

Invite calm — not silence, just calm.
Sit together.
Let the child know this is a "Jesus moment."

• 2. Read slowly.

Let lines breathe.
Let the child imagine.
Let their eyes look away as they picture what they hear.

• 3. Ask Wonder Questions.

Not "What did you learn?"
But questions that open imagination:

• "What part of this felt most true to you?"

• "Where do you think Jesus was standing in this story?"

• "What do you think His face looked like?"

• "How do you think His voice sounded?"

Let them explore.
Let them be free.

• 4. Practice the Declaration.

Speak it aloud together.
Children love rhythm and repetition.
This is how truth slowly becomes instinct.

• 5. Say the Prayer Gently.

Let the child speak if they want.
If they don't, speak for them.
Some children listen their prayers before they say them.

3. HOW CHILDREN EXPERIENCE JESUS

Children don't meet Jesus through long explanations.
They meet Him through:

- A story that makes Him feel real

- A picture that makes Him feel near

- A moment that makes Him feel gentle

- A prayer that makes Him feel listening

- A verse that makes Him feel strong

Your goal is to help them **feel** Him before they try to understand Him.

Understanding grows later.
Trust grows now.

4. THREE DAILY PRACTICES TO CULTIVATE

This book introduces three spiritual habits designed for children:

1. A DAILY MEMORY VERSE MOMENT

Keep it short.

Keep it soft.
Make it joyful.

Goal:
God's words settle into the child's heart the way seeds settle into good soil.

Suggested rhythm:
"Let's say our verse one time in a calm voice...
one time in a happy voice...
one time in a whisper Jesus can hear."

2. A DAILY TALK WITH JESUS

Let this be flexible.
Let it be natural.

Jesus wants real conversation, not performance.

Some children will talk a lot.
Some will whisper little words.
Some will simply sit quietly and that counts too.

The goal is not words — the goal is **awareness**.

3. A DAILY DECLARATION

Declarations build identity.
They teach the child to speak truth over themselves.

Say it slow.
Let them feel the words.

Each declaration in this book is written to anchor a child's confidence in Jesus.

5. HOW TO HANDLE A CHILD'S QUESTIONS

Children will ask deep questions in tiny voices:

- "Why did Jesus die?"

- "Where is Heaven?"

- "Does Jesus see me when I'm scared?"

- "Can Jesus hear my thoughts?"

- "Does Jesus get sad?"

- "Why can't I see Jesus with my eyes?"

Don't rush to give big answers.
Give simple truth, spoken slowly:

- "Jesus died because He loves you."

- "Yes, Jesus sees you when you're scared."

- "Jesus can hear every thought you think."

- "Jesus never leaves your side."

- "One day we will see Him with our eyes too."

Children aren't looking for explanations.
They're looking for **assurance**.

6. KEEPING JESUS IN THE CHILD'S IMAGINATION

The imagination is a child's prayer room.

Encourage them to picture Jesus:

- Walking beside them

- Laughing with them

- Holding their hand

- Sitting with them in silence

- Listening at bedtime

- Standing beside their bed when they wake up

- Smiling when they sing

- Comforting them when they cry

The goal is to make Jesus **somebody they know**,
not **somebody they only learn about**.

7. BLESSING THE CHILD AT THE END OF EACH READING

End each reading with a short blessing spoken over them:

"Jesus is with you.
Jesus loves you.
Jesus watches over you.
Jesus enjoys being with you.
Jesus will never let you go."

These small blessings shape a child's spiritual future.

They are how identity takes root.

8. FINAL WORD TO THE GROWN-UP

You are planting seeds that will grow long after this book closes.

Every page you read,
every prayer you whisper,
every declaration you speak with your child
it all builds a foundation that Jesus Himself will strengthen
throughout their life.

You are not just teaching a book.
You are introducing a Person.
And that Person — Jesus —
will walk with this child forever.

PRAYER

for Nationalisation into the
Kingdom of Heaven

Scriptural Foundation:

- *John 3:3 – "Jesus answered and said to him, 'Most assuredly, I say to you, unless one is born again, he cannot see the kingdom of God.'"*

- *Philippians 3:20 – "For our citizenship is in heaven, from which we also eagerly wait for the Savior, the Lord Jesus Christ."*

- *Ephesians 2:19 – "Now therefore you are no longer strangers and foreigners, but fellow citizens with the saints and members of the household of God."*

- *Colossians 1:13 – "He has delivered us from the power of darkness and conveyed us into the kingdom of the Son of His love."*

- *Romans 10:9 – "That if you confess with your mouth the Lord Jesus and believe in your heart that God has raised Him from the dead, you will be saved."*

Righteous Judge of Heaven and Earth,

I come before Your throne, the **throne of Grace** in **the Court of Heaven**, in the name of Jesus Christ, my Lord and Saviour. I stand by the power of His precious blood, which has **redeemed me** and **bought my salvation**. I come humbly and boldly, desiring to be **nationalised into the Kingdom of Heaven**—to become a **true citizen of Your heavenly realm.**

Father, Your Word declares in **John 3:3** that **unless one is born again**, they cannot see the Kingdom of God. Today, **I renounce any citizenship** I once held in this world and any **ties to the powers of darkness**. I acknowledge that I have been **transferred from the kingdom of darkness into the Kingdom of the Son** of Your love (*Colossians 1:13*). I declare that I am no longer a stranger or foreigner, but a **fellow citizen with the saints** and a member of the household of God (*Ephesians 2:19*).

Lord Jesus, I believe with all my heart that You are the **Son of the living God**, that You died for my sins and rose again to grant me eternal life (**Romans 10:9**). I now receive You as my **personal Savior, my Redeemer, the only Way, the Truth**, and **the Life**. You are the **Door to the Father's heart** and the only **path to salvation**. I do not want to **perish** with the world, but to **live eternally with You.**

At this moment, I [Your Full Name] solemnly, sincerely, and truthfully affirm my love, my seriousness, and my desire to follow You and serve You in **holiness and righteousness**. I pledge my full allegiance to You, O King of kings and Lord of lords. I give my loyalty to the third Heaven and honour its **rights and freedoms**. I desire to settle with You, **Lord Jesus**. I repent of the way I have **lived my life and of all my sins**. Take over **my heart and my destiny**. Save me, cleanse me, and change me.

I beseech that You **seal my heavenly citizenship today**. Let the record of **my new identity** be **registered in the Court of Heaven**. Write my name in the **Lamb's Book of Life**, and erase it from the **book of death and judgment**. Let every **legal claim the enemy** has over my past be **cancelled** and **rendered powerless by the blood of Jesus**.

Lord, I am ready to walk the path of **righteousness and holiness**. I cast all **my cares and all of myself upon You**, for You care for me and loved me and laid Your life as the Lamb slain from **the foundation of the world**. Let Your **will be done** in my life as it is in Heaven.

By Your blood, I now receive eternal life. I proclaim that I am a **new creature**. By the word of Your testimony, I am made free indeed. **Fill me and baptize me** with the **Holy Ghost and fire**. Thank You, Lord Jesus, for giving me the right and the power to become a child of God, born **not of flesh but of the Spirit**, according to **the new covenant sealed in Your blood**.

I believe **You died** for me, and on the **third day**, You rose again. You are now seated at the right hand of the **Father in glory**, and I receive You as the Lord of my life. Through You, I have **received grace, peace, forgiveness, and eternal inheritance**. I stand holy, blameless, and without fault before the **Court of Heaven** because of the **righteousness imputed to me through Your sacrifice**.

Now, I **declare that the power of sin, death, and Satan—including the grave**—has been **broken over my life**. I walk in the eternal victory of the Cross. From this day forward, I will never look back. Backward—never. Forward—forever.

Degree and Declare: I am a citizen of Heaven. I live for Your Kingdom. **I walk in Your authority and power**. I receive the **full inheritance of health, peace, righteousness, Wealth, and provision, even eternal life**.

In Jesus' mighty name, I pray.

Amen.

EPILOGUE

When a child meets Jesus,
something quiet and beautiful begins inside them
a light that doesn't fade,
a friendship that doesn't break,
a song that keeps singing even when the room grows still.

This book has been a small doorway into that friendship.
A whisper of His love.
A first glimpse of His smile.

But Jesus does not stay in the pages.
He walks with your child into every part of life
into the places they laugh,
into the moments they feel unsure,
into the times they need courage,
and into the days that stretch wide with joy.

The story continues now
in your home,
in your child's heart,
and in all the tiny, ordinary moments
where Jesus makes Himself known in ways small eyes can see and
small hands can hold.

This isn't the end.

It is the breath before the next chapter,
the glow before the next sunrise,
the gentle reminder that Jesus whispers still:

"I am with you always."

AFTERWORD

You have reached the last page of this book,
but not the last page of your child's story with Jesus.

In many ways, this is only the beginning.

With every chapter, every prayer, every little whisper during "Talk With Jesus" time, a seed has been planted;quietly, simply, and beautifully. These early moments of meeting Jesus are treasures that grow slowly, like sunlight stretching across a morning sky.

If your child has smiled, wondered, asked a question, or reached out their tiny heart in any way while reading this book, then something wonderful is already happening:
they are learning that Jesus is real, Jesus is kind, and Jesus is theirs.

As they grow, the questions will grow.
The understanding will grow.
And the relationship will grow too: steady, joyful, anchored in love.

Thank you for taking this journey with your child.
Thank you for reading aloud, pausing, imagining, and gently guiding their heart toward the One who loves them most.

May the sweetness of these early steps become a foundation for every step that comes after.
And may Jesus—faithful, gentle, and forever near walk with your child all the days of their life.

With hope and gratitude,
Anthony Mwangi

ACKNOWLEDGEMENT

Lorem ipsum dolor sit amet, consectetur adipiscing elit, sed do eiusmod tempor incididunt ut labore et dolore magna aliqua. Ut enim ad minim veniam, quis nostrud exercitation ullamco laboris.

ABOUT THE AUTHOR

Anthony Mwangi

Anthony Mwangi is a prophetic architect of kingdom intelligence, an inspired voice committed to restoring ancient pathways and operationalising spiritual truth for the modern believer. His work fuses lyrical revelation with disciplined biblical scholarship, driving a strategic mandate: to awaken identity, rebuild covenant consciousness, and align nations with the government of God.

Guided by the Spirit and anchored in the King James Scripture, Anthony's teachings weave together the seven dimensions of the Word: Spiritology, Soulogy, Physiology, Theology, Chronology, Typology, and Technology into a unified framework for transformation. His forward-facing mission is to empower a generation to stand in the heavenly courtroom, navigate spiritual ecosystems with precision, and reclaim the rest of God as their operational baseline.

With humility and relentless pursuit, Anthony curates prophetic blueprints such as The Sabbath Is the Spirit, Stones of Fire, and the emerging series on spiritual warfare and kingdom governance. His voice is both ancient and new—rooted in the dust of Eden, yet calibrated for the strategic demands of the last days. He writes and teaches so that every reader may discover the original design encoded in their spirit and walk boldly in the glory for which they were created.

THE WHIRRING CHILDREN

The Whirring Children Series champions the next generation with stories that hum with wonder, truth, and holy possibility. Each book helps young hearts discover who Jesus is, how His Word speaks, and why their lives carry divine design.

Built for early learners yet rich with spiritual depth, this series equips children to grow in identity, courage, and Christ-cantered thinking. Every title is a small ignition point—sparking joy, stirring curiosity, and shaping a lifelong rhythm of walking with God.

From creation to prayer...
from purpose to worship...
from Bible discovery to daily living...
The Whirring Children Series builds a foundation of faith that keeps turning, lifting, and lighting their steps as they grow.

This is more than storytelling.
It's formation.
It's alignment.
It's the future God is cultivating in His little ones—one book at a time.

Book 1 — Who Is Jesus?

Theme: Meeting Jesus for the first time
Core Outcome: The child knows Jesus loves them and is always with them
Features:

- Simple gospel story
- First memory verse
- First prayer of belonging
- Daily "Talk With Jesus" activity

Book 2 — My First Bible Adventure

Theme: Introduction to Scripture
Core Outcome: The child sees the Bible as a treasure from God
Features:
- Seven major Bible stories
- Bible treasure map
- How to open, read, and remember Scripture

Book 3 — I Can Talk To God

Theme: Prayer
Core Outcome: Prayer becomes natural, easy, and joyful
Features:
- Types of prayer
- Jesus' teaching on prayer
- Evening and morning prayer practices

Book 4 — God Made Me Special

Theme: Identity
Core Outcome: The child knows they were designed with purpose
Features:
- Affirmations
- Psalm 139 simplified
- Gifts, talents, emotions in God's plan

Book 5 — God Is Always With Me

Theme: God's presence
Core Outcome: Emotional security and spiritual awareness

Features:
- Courage
- Comfort
- Peace
- Angelic protection explained gently

Book 6 — Learning God's Love

Theme: God's character
Core Outcome: The heart becomes rooted in love, not fear
Features:
- God's love in Jesus
- Loving others
- How love transforms behaviour

Book 7 — The Big Story Of Creation

Theme: God as Creator
Core Outcome: Awe, responsibility, gratitude
Features:
- Genesis simplified
- Earth care
- Purpose in creation

Book 8 — Jesus My Shepherd

Theme: Guidance
Core Outcome: Trust in the leadership of Christ
Features:
- Psalm 23 simplified
- Making good choices
- Listening to God

Book 9 — I Belong To God's Family

Theme: Community & church

Core Outcome: Understanding church as a place of love and unity
Features:
– What is the Church?
– Friendship
– Serving others

Book 10 — Let Your Light Shine

Theme: Character & behaviour
Core Outcome: The child understands their life is a testimony
Features:
– Kindness, honesty, courage
– The fruit of the Spirit in child language

Book 11 — God Gives Me Strength

Theme: Resilience & spiritual growth
Core Outcome: Learning how to face challenges with God
Features:
– Overcoming fear
– Trying again
– God's promises for strength

Book 12 — Following Jesus Every Day

Theme: Daily discipleship
Core Outcome: A lifestyle shaped around Jesus
Features:
– Morning routine with God
– Sharing faith
– Living like Jesus at home and school
– Graduation page with blessing

BOOKS BY THIS AUTHOR

The Armour Of Light: Unlocking The Mystery Of Divine Warfare

In the last days, the battlefield is no longer fought with swords and spears, but with light, truth, and the Spirit. The Armour of Light: Unlocking the Mystery of Divine Warfare is a prophetic unveiling of God's end-time strategy for His chosen remnant.

This masterpiece reveals the hidden dimensions of the Word of God and the power of the Holy Spirit as the true armour that clothes, protects, and empowers the believer. Through spiritology, soulogy, physiology, and theology, the mystery of warfare is unfolded—showing how the Sabbath is God's dwelling place, the Courtroom of Heaven is His battlefield, and the Bride is His warrior.

Drawing from ancient truths and prophetic revelations, Anthony Mwangi — the BRANCH seated in Zion — uncovers the role of man in God's eternal judgment, the secret of Christ's blood as the light of warfare, and the revelation of the 7-dimensional Word as the weapon that disarms the dragon, the beast, and the false prophet.

This book is not just a teaching, but a weapon in itself. It equips the end-time believer to stand clothed in fire, sealed by the Spirit, and ready to triumph in the last battle.

If you are called to be part of the remnant, this is your manual of divine warfare.

The True Church (Ekklesia): The Undisputed Government Of Heaven On Earth

he Church was never designed to be a passive audience. It was crafted to be a governing body; Heaven's operational command centre on the earth.

This prophetic masterpiece unveils the Church in her original mandate: a ruling, legislative, fire-crowned government seated in Christ, built to administer righteousness, execute divine justice, and steward the expansion of the Kingdom with unshakeable authority.

Moving beyond institutional religion, this book repositions the reader inside the architectural blueprint of God's eternal design, where the Ekklesia stands as Heaven's governing senate, the Lamb's undefeated Heavyweight Government operating in light, truth, and dominion.

Each chapter pulls you deeper into the designer realm of the Word, where identity becomes structure and revelation becomes strategy. You will discover:

The true governmental nature of the Church
How sons legislate from Zion through rest, not striving
Why hell cannot contend with a people aligned to the Throne
How the 7-Dimensional Word of God equips believers for rule
The rise of Kingdom coalitions, watchtowers, and councils
The architecture of divine order that establishes peace without end
This is not just a teaching; it is a governmental activation. A call to rise, build, legislate, and stand in your ordained post within Heaven's expanding Kingdom.

For reformers, intercessors, apostolic builders, prophetic architects, and every believer hungry to move beyond survival into governance, this book is your blueprint.

Step into the council.
Stand in the light.
Take your seat in the Undisputed Government of the Lamb.

Sabbath: The Name Of The Holy Spirit — God's Covenant Protocol For The Last Days

This book unveils a groundbreaking revelation: the Sabbath is the Name, Seal, and Rest of the Holy Spirit, and the end-time Church cannot walk in covenant power without understanding this identity. Drawing from the 7-Dimensional Word of God, this work decodes the Sabbath as God's ancient–future protocol — the original sign of His presence, the governing code of His kingdom, and the prophetic mark that distinguishes His remnant in the last days.

You will discover how the Sabbath reveals God's hidden Name, aligns the mind with divine order, and positions the body as the dwelling place where the Spirit rests. From Eden's first seventh-day revelation to the sealed remnant of Revelation, this book demonstrates that to hallow the Sabbath is to hallow His Name, and that the restoration of Sabbath order is the restoration of God's government on earth.

Packed with visionary insights, prophetic typology, and a full blueprint for spiritual formation, this book equips believers to:

Understand the Sabbath as the signature identity of the Holy Spirit

Discern the covenant seal that separates truth from deception in the last days

Rebuild the altar of rest in the mind, heart, and body

Walk in the rhythm, protection, and judgment of God's kingdom order

Stand in Zion as those who have entered His Rest

This is not merely theology — it is kingdom strategy.
A call to return.
A summons to alignment.
A preparation for the remnant.

SABBATH: The Name of the Holy Spirit is your guide to reclaiming God's original covenant protocol, and stepping into the Rest that marks His people for the final generation.